Jewelry
doll

Make bracelets, necklaces, anklets, and more!

American Girl®

Contents

Jeweler School

Chains

Plastic Cord

Hemp

Floss

Memory Wire

Ribbon

Paper Cord/Earrings

Dear Doll Lover,

Surprise your doll with beaded bracelets, *fancy necklaces*, adorable anklets, and more!

These *easy-to-make jewelry* pieces will suit any occasion. Braid a hemp bracelet for a barbecue. Decorate a ribbon choker for a fancy dinner. *Design a tiara* for a night at the theater. Or simply press on *rhinestone earrings* to accent a glamorous hairstyle.

It's all about fashion flair—and instant fun!

*Your Friends
at American Girl*

Getting Started

Ready to start styling? Learn about your kit supplies!

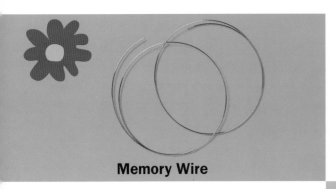

Memory Wire

Memory wire will keep its shape, so you don't need a clasp to hold it together. Stretch the wire around the doll with the opening in back, and the wire will snap into place. Ask an adult to bend the ends with pliers. Be careful with pointy ends—they could scratch.

Braid, twist, or knot floss to create different jewelry designs. Mix and match colors to accent your doll's outfits.

Embroidery Floss

Ribbon & Rhinestone Earrings

The ends of the ribbon can sometimes fray, but it will help if you cut each end into a V.

The stickiness on your rhinestone earrings won't last forever, so use them for special occasions.

Unroll and gently tug the ends of the paper cord to make it flatter and more flexible. Pinch the ends together to make points.

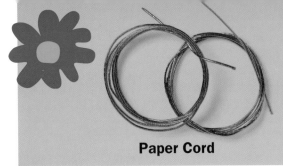

Paper Cord

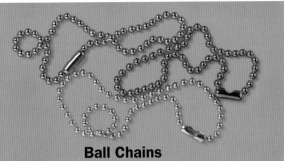

Ball Chains

Make necklaces or bracelets with ball chains. Slip a single ball at the end of the ball chain into the clasp and tug to close.

Plastic cord will stretch over your doll's hands. Just be sure not to stretch it too much or it might break. Hemp tends to stay curled, but wetting it and laying it straight to dry helps.

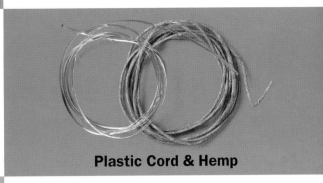

Plastic Cord & Hemp

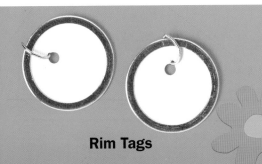

Rim Tags

To learn how to turn rim tags into charms, read the directions on page 22.

Style Smarts

Read these tips before you start!

• **Ask an adult!** When you see this symbol, always ask an adult to help you.

• **Think before you cut.** Your kit supplies are limited, so be careful when you cut a chain or a piece of hemp, ribbon, or cord. Make sure that you won't want to use it as a longer piece later.

• **Don't get your jewelry wet.** Water could ruin your jewelry designs—especially charms.

• **Create some jewelry for two.** Make the same jewelry for yourself. You can purchase extra supplies at craft or bead stores.

• **Bead troubles?** If you're having trouble threading cord or floss through a bead, try poking the end of a paper clip through the bead to clear the hole.

Doll Jewelry Dimensions

A finished doll necklace is about 8 inches long.

A finished choker is $5\frac{1}{2}$ inches long.

A finished bracelet is $3\frac{3}{4}$ inches long.

A finished anklet is $4\frac{1}{2}$ inches long.

Here's How

Follow these simple instructions to make a loop, knots, and a braid.

End Loop

Use an end loop as a clasp.

1. Fold strand in half.

2. Tie knot at folded end, leaving a tiny end loop.

3. Pull tight.

Permanent Closure Knot

Tying on to an end loop makes a permanent closure.

1. Slip end of 1 strand through end loop.

2. Tie other strand in a double knot.

Removable Closure Knot

This removable knot fits into an end loop.

1. Tie all strands together into a knot.

2. Trim end short.

For a clasp, slip knot through an end loop.

Braiding

Braid for fun jewelry!

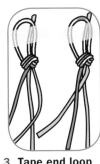

1. Cut 2 strands of floss or hemp so that 1 strand is twice as long as the other.

2. Fold long strand in half, then tie an end loop.

3. Tape end loop to table. Cross right strand over center strand, and then left strand over new center strand.

4. Repeat until braid is the length you want. Tie permanent or removable closure knot. Trim ends.

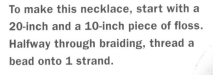

To make this necklace, start with a 20-inch and a 10-inch piece of floss. Halfway through braiding, thread a bead onto 1 strand.

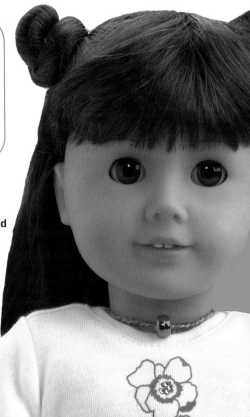

Charming Chains

Turn plain chains into eye-catching necklaces with these simple ideas.

Layered Lengths

Start with 3 different chain colors. Ask an adult to cut $\frac{1}{2}$ inch off one chain color and $1\frac{1}{2}$ inches off another color. Put all 3 chains on your doll.

Twisted Spiral

Tape the ends of 2 different-colored chains to a table, then twist them together. Pull off the tape, but hold the chains in place until you put them on your doll.

Anklets and Bracelets

Ask an adult to cut chains to the correct length for anklets and bracelets.

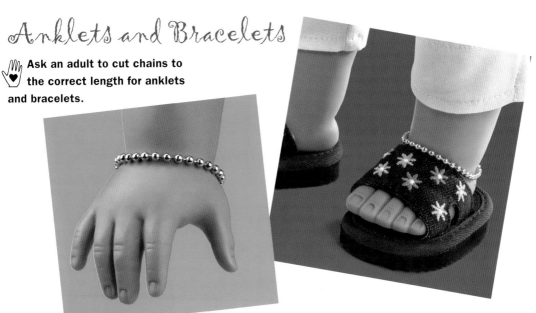

Fashion Necklaces

Get together with friends and design your own doll jewelry.

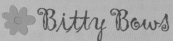

Bitty Bows

For an eye-catching necklace, tie small pieces of thin ribbon between the balls on a chain. Trim ribbon.

Pretty Pendant

Create a stylish pendant by sliding a pretty bead onto a chain. Try a different bead when you change your doll's outfit.

Charmer

Accent an outfit with the perfect charm. (Learn how to make a charm on page 22.) Tip: Press a sticker to the back and the charm is reversible!

Wrap 'n' Snap

Wrap 3 loops of paper cord tightly around the end of a chain to hold the cord on the chain. Continue to wrap the cord around the chain, finishing with 3 more tight loops.

Beaded Style

Clear plastic cord lets your favorite bead colors shine through!

Mix and Match

For a bracelet, cut a 9-inch piece of plastic cord. Thread on beads for $3\frac{3}{4}$ inches. (Tip: Use a binder clip to hold one end of the cord so the beads won't slip off while you're stringing them on.) Knot ends, bringing the beads together. Add a dab of clear-drying glue to the knot. Let dry. Trim ends.

Headband Sparkle

For a headband, start with 14 inches of plastic cord. Tie a knot $5\frac{1}{2}$ inches from one end. String on 3 inches of beads. Tie another knot to hold the beads in place. Try the headband on your doll to find the best place to tie an end knot, then tie ends together. Add a drop of glue to the end knot. Trim ends.

Tip: If knot loosens, ask someone to pull it tight while you dab on glue.

Hip in Hemp

Create a retro hippie look with natural-fiber jewelry!

Necklace

Fold a 20-inch strand of hemp in half. Make an end loop (see page 8). Tie a knot 4 inches from the end loop. Slide on a pony bead, and make another knot next to the bead. Make a removable closure knot (see page 8) at the end.

Bracelet

Use the same technique described above, but start with a 16-inch piece of hemp, and tie the first knot 2 inches from the end loop.

Anklet

Braid 3 strands of hemp to create a very cool anklet, then tie it on.

Belt

A belt starts with a 48-inch piece of hemp. Make an end loop. Then every few inches tie a knot, slip on a bead, and tie another knot. For a cool closure, slide a bead onto the end and knot again.

Loop Pendants

Making this necklace is as easy as can be with one loop—or three!

Little Loops

Mix it up! Style a necklace with three beads on one loop or one bead on each of three loops.

1. Fold 15 inches of floss in half. Slide on 3 beads at fold.

2. Ask someone to place a pencil over beads while you tie a knot. Remove pencil and you'll have a loop. Try on doll, then tie in back. Trim ends.

Option: Slide a single bead onto floss, and knot as above. Tie another beaded loop to left and another to right of first loop.

Note: After removing pencil, don't pull on knot or loop will tighten around bead.

20

Give a toy pup a cute collar and leash or
make a trendy anklet by tying beads on floss.

Fancy Floss

Give floss a fashion twist with these nifty knots.

Wrist Twist

Shown in photo at far left.

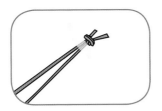

1. Start with two 1-foot strands of floss. Knot ends together, then tape knot to worktable.

2. Twist floss to other end. Press down on middle of bracelet and fold ends together.

3. Holding ends tightly, let go of middle. Bracelet will twist on itself! Tie a knot closure.

Knotty & Nice

Shown in photo at near left.

1. Start with 3 strands of floss. Fold 1 strand in half, then tie an end loop. Tape end loop to worktable. Braid for 1 inch.

2. Combine 2 strands into 1 strand, then use single strand to make a "4" shape. Pull end of single strand through "4" as shown.

3. Pull knot snugly to top. Repeat step 2 until you have $1\frac{1}{2}$ inches of spiral knots. Braid for 1 more inch. Tie a knot closure.

Friendship Charms

Create a charm for your doll and one for you with this simple design!

For a charm: press a sticker from page 33 onto a rim tag. Ask an adult to make a hole in the paper at the top using a pin or micro hole punch. Open a jump ring, slip it through the hole, and close it.

For a necklace, ask an adult to use jewelry pliers to bend an end loop on a piece of memory wire as shown at right. Slide on the charm. Have an adult make another end loop. Repeat to make yourself a matching bracelet!

Purr Fect

Beaded Chokers

Find a reason each season to create a new necklace style.

✸ Fall Colors

Slide autumn-colored beads onto wire—perfect for long-sleeved shirts and sweaters.

✸ Winter Ice

String icy-colored beads on memory wire for holiday and special-event outfits.

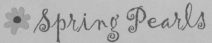

❋ Spring Pearls

Treat your doll to floating pearls. Add a dab of clear-drying glue on the memory wire where you want a pearl-colored bead to rest. Repeat.

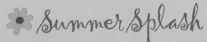

❋ Summer Splash

Reflect sapphire seas by mixing dark blue pony beads with light blue seed beads on memory wire.

Ribbon Twists

Tie on organza ribbon to create easy and elegant neckwear.

Cheer Charm

Create a charm following the directions on page 22. Slide it onto a ribbon, then tie the ribbon in back.

Organza Scarf

Slip a pony bead onto each end of a ribbon, then tie double knots at both ends. Tie the scarf around your doll's neck using a half-knot.

Beaded Choker

Slide 3 pony beads onto a ribbon. Tie the ribbon in back. Space out beads for one look, or slide beads together to get another style!

Bow Tie

Wrap a ribbon around your doll's neck twice, then tie a knot in front. Cut a V from each ribbon end.

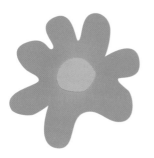

Crown Jewels

A tiara and rhinestone earrings will make any doll look like royalty.

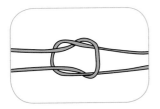

1. Start with 2 blue paper cords from kit. Bend them in half to make loops. Put loops inside each other as shown above.

2. Pinch top of loops at about same height to make points. Tape down points.

3. Thread 1 pink paper cord through loops as shown above.

4. Loop each end of pink strand around bottom blue strands on each side. Points might move, so keep them centered.

5. Untape 1 side, and make a 4-inch braid. Repeat on other side. Trim ends and wrap with clear tape. Slip tiara into your doll's hair.

Don't forget your "diamond" or "aquamarine" earrings! To apply, peel them off the sticker sheet and stick them to your doll's earlobes.

Make a doll-sized jewelry holder! Glue felt onto a small corkboard. Let dry, then press in colorful pushpins. Press on adhesive foam stickers, if desired. To hang, make holes at top with a hole punch. Thread a ribbon through holes, and knot ends. Hang jewelry on pushpins.

Show us your designs!

Send photos to:

Doll Jewelry Editor
American Girl
8400 Fairway Place
P.O. Box 620998
Middleton, WI 53562

(Photos can't be returned.
All comments and suggestions
received by Pleasant Company Publications
may be used without compensation
or acknowledgment.)

Here are some other American Girl books you might like:

❑ I read it.

❑ I read it.

❑ I read it.

❑ I read it.

❑ I read it.

❑ I read it.